The Power Of Goal Setting

LEARN WHY DO PEOPLE FAIL, WHY GOALS ARE IMPORTANT, AND HOW TO SET, AND ACHIEVE THEM?

Vikram Brahma

Table Of Content

Acknowledgement

This book couldn't have happened without the support of many individuals in my life. First of all, I am grateful to omnipotent God for allowing me to work on my dream projects and passion as a digital entrepreneur. I am thankful for digital platforms and softwares like MS Word (Microsoft) and Google Doc (Google). Thanks to them, now we can write digitally and save a lot of time. I am also grateful to many online publishing sites like Amazon Kindle or iBook or Kobo or Google Play and many more for allowing us to publish our books in the digital format. I am also indebted to canva.com for providing a valuable yet simple online platform so I could design my book cover easily.

Apart from this, I am thankful to my beautiful editor and business partner, Ms. Bidinta Boro for reading and editing my book as many times as I liked. She is an extremely talented and hard-working individual, who can easily translate and edit. By the way, we run one YouTube channel together and if you like to visit our channel then check this link www.youtube.com/youreawesome. I am sure we will work together for many years as a solid team and let's grow our agency and work together.

Let me share my short story as to how I became an author from a writer. I have the passion and I always wanted to write like a pro. I have already written and published more than 140 articles for the Hubpages forum https://hubpages.com/@talesofvikram. I have also written many articles for my blog related to North-East India. I have been writing articles for my clients and making money out of it. One day while scrolling on Facebook, I came across one advertisement related to one free webinar on the topic of how to become an author in 30 days. I immediately joined the webinar as I always wanted to become a writer and an author as it was my long-cherished dream. Since I managed to develop a habit of writing almost 1000+ words from many months, I realized that this is God's sign and as they say, rest is history.

My acknowledgement will not be complete if I will not mention my guru's name in my books. Let me write a few lines for him. My coach, Mr. Som Bathla is an accomplished author/authorpreneur himself, and he has written and published over 20 books on online platforms including Amazon Kindle. I learned every aspect of writing a book and self-publishing from his course. I am indebted that he introduced me to this amazing path of writing and self-publishing books online. After joining his online course I could visualize several possibilities as an author/authorpreneur. Let's hope for the best.

I couldn't have able to start my journey as an author and a digital entrepreneur without the support of my lovely parents, Mr. Kabi Ranjan Brahma (ex-DIG, C. R.P.F) and Mrs. Renu Brahma (ex-school teacher and a proud homemaker). They gave me enough time and space for an office within our house without worrying about rent or electricity bills. I hope I have been using our home space in the best possible manner. Now, I work independently from home and just enjoying every minute of my digital work. I am also grateful to my clients who never pressurized me to work only on their projects on an urgent basis and allowed me to take some time and complete my book as per my scheduled.

Life will have no real meaning without close friends and I am really lucky to have some close friends. They are the ones who are supporting me mentally in every part of my journey as an author without directly involving in my work. When you start your unknown journey usually no one will support you but I was lucky to have a few close friends with whom I could share my ups and downs. I always asked them to support me mentally and they kept their ears open whenever I shared my plans, ideas, visions, projects, or goals. I love to discuss ideas and my next goals with them. And they like and listen to me because I proved to them it is possible to earn money by working entirely from home. I started every project which I discussed with them verbally in the last year be it blogging, my writing career, YouTuber journey, a stock investor, podcaster, and now as an author. I hope I can keep their faith alive in me always.

Without delay let me share my friends' names without any particular order. They are Mrs. Jenteka Bargayary Brahma, Ms. Nandita Das, Ms. Bidinta Boro, Ms. Bwhwithi Boro, Ms. Mithinga Boro, Ms. Dipika Brahma, Ms. Dipshika Goswami, Ms. Nilanjana Bhuyan, Mrs. Rwmwi Rongjali Narzary, Mrs. Nijira Kochary, Mr. Gopal Singh Negi, Mr. Parag Tanna, Mr. Yashwant Wala, Mr. Sudip Shah, Mr. Prashant Pillai, Mr. Abhishek Ghavri, Mr. Ajay Kumar Mishra, Mr. Sumon Mukherjee, Ms. Maytree Mazumder, Ms. Sonam Prasad, Ms. Monica Raj Undrajavarapu, Mr. Syed Hameed (ex-teacher), Mrs. Annapurna Seshadri (ex-teacher), Mrs. Jagadeeswari Krishnamsetty (ex-teacher), and Mrs. Annapurna Suddapalli (ex-teacher).

Finally, I want to thank thousands of my connections on my social media profiles be it on Facebook or LinkedIn or

Twitter or Instagram or WhatsApp, or YouTube combined. They are all great sources of inspiration and I learn many things by observing them. I love to share motivational content with them in the form of written posts, videos, or podcasts. I hope they are also learning as well as enjoying and they are very much part of my entrepreneurship journey. I couldn't have grown much without their feedbacks, support, and love. They are awesome and I love them all always.

"Having seen multiple failures in life, both professional and personal level, now I live every day to achieve my set goals"
By Vikram Brahma, Author, Writer, Blogger, YouTuber

....

Introduction

Contrary to popular belief and the standard set by the school, colleges, and society, failures are an inevitable part of life. Human history and society over and over again has proved that this major component of human evolution cannot be ruled out by any chance. Those who desire to achieve great success in life shouldn't be upset by some losses. When we face hardship and difficulties in life either we lose our balance or we bounce back in life with more force and energy. And the choice is always ours. Failure and success are the two parts of the same coin. I assume you have decided to read this book with the one and only purpose to learn how to set and achieve your goals.

To give true meaning and accuracy to this book, I will love to share my part of failures and success with my lovely readers. I want to show you that it is normal to encounter failures in life. And why do I believe setting goals are the most important factor to live a meaningful life. I want to prove to you that it is possible to set goals and achieve them. My own journey as a writer and author is one such example and we are going to see that in detail. Over the years, I have closely observed many successful people and I have noticed some unique behavior about them. I have read many success stories of great people and we are lucky to discuss them. In my personal opinion, I highly support that there is an urgent need to teach the student community about - how to set goals in life and what tools are needed to achieve them? And even more than that they should be taught – how to set meaningful and right kinds of goals and achieve them?

When I started my career at the young age of 21, I was like anyone else – a little bit clueless, but full of energy and hungry for success. I thought I have to simply pass my post-graduation and I will join some good advertising agency for life and ultimately, my career and life are all set. Now, read further carefully and you will agree with me. Nowadays, when I meet young fellows and I ask them what they wanted to do in life, they mostly tell me about their higher studies goals and their dream of getting a job in some govt. department or in the corporate world or public sector banks. In my own small town in Assam (India), students mostly prefer either govt. jobs, contractual work under govt. or will like to open some shop. If you will ever visit my town you will notice a hundred small restaurants and roadside food stalls everywhere. Then I ask them further questions, like - what they really wanted to do in life? Have you set some goals in your life? Well, most art students would reply – they wanted to do a Bachelor of Education (B.Ed), so they can get jobs as a permanent teacher. When I ask the same question to the science students some of them reply with the same answer. And although there is a commerce college in our small town but then there is no industry or corporate houses available to hire them. They too lookout for some jobs in the govt. department. But I am also sure this is the exact scenario in almost every small town of India and any other part of the world.

Sometimes, I don't understand and find it a little funny (yes, now I laugh a lot to keep my health in good condition) that when there is a problem related to how to create more jobs then why no institute actually teaches more about this subject. Yes, I do personally believe that till the time our education system will emphasize more on creating job lookers rather than job creators then this problem will persist. I once heard that education is the key to success. By implementing that knowledge one can find true meaning in life. But despite that why do so many people are suffering and upset about their life? Did our education system actually failed us (millions and billions of people) or did we actually failed to use the education system properly? Well, I don't have to answer these questions because if you look around your situation you will get the right answer. ***So, now the question arises what are the real keys to success and happiness?*** Well, I would say – I am a seeker of knowledge, philosopher and I am an author, so I would try (honestly) to answer this question with my limited knowledge which I have able to gather in the last three decades of my existence on this planet called - mother earth. In short, here is the key to ultimate success and happiness:

a) Invest time, moncy, and effort to find what you really love to do

b) Learn everything possible about your love (work)

c) Invest time, money, and effort to build a business around your love (work)

d) Once you grow share your knowledge (happily) and teach others in return of money. So, you can make more money and help others to grow

e) Repeat the entire system as much as possible and master it

Now if you are thinking about how to find your love (work) and passion then the answer is first learn to observe yourself. Don't follow any friends or social norms.

Present and future are all about you and what you will do and how you will be known for. Remember when you will try to be different you may fail multiple times. But don't lose hope. I have told my students millions of times that this universe is ready to give you anything. But first, it will test you in his own unique ways to know whether you are worthy of that success or not. That test can happen on any day and in any circumstances. By hard work and dedication if you will pass those rigorous life's tests successfully then welcome to the world of successful individuals.

What Should You Expect From This Book?

This book contains information related to why do we need to set goals in life, why people fail despite goal setting? How can we set goals, progress in life, and achieve our goals? I have added a particular chapter – why do people fail despite goal setting because we should know the actual reasons and learn how to overcome them. Anyone who will read this book will understand the psychology and mindset of a successful person. Yes, there is a direct relationship between mindset and goal setting.

You will find that this book is written in a very simple language that even a 7th standard kid can understand. Apart from this, overall the book contains five chapters, and each chapter is divided into different sub-topics, so it will be very easy to read and digest. In fact, as per my own experience, you can even complete reading this book within the next three to five days. Remember my core idea for writing this book is to make you believe that setting goals in life are as important as breathing.

Before you apply any system make sure you are mentally ready. I have written and shared many times that there is a common belief among successful people that achieving the goals of life depends upon the mindset of the individual person. If you are committed then you can be sure of achieving your goals in life. Plan it and take action. I rest my argument with this hope that after reading this book you will be more active in finding your true love and romance (work) in life.

So, let's get started.

Chapter 1

Why Setting The Right Goals Are Important?

"Mindset is a skill. It can be taught and learned."
By Russel Wilson, American Football Player

....

Before we move further and deep dive, let us concentrate on the most important aspect related to goal setting. If you wanted to know why setting goals are important for life then this book is certainly not for you. Well, did I just surprised you with my words or sentence? Ok, now let's read it one more time. If you really wanted to know why **setting the right goals** is important for life then this book is definitely for you. Yes, there is something called goals and then there is something called setting the right kind of goals. Usually, we get trapped due to our ignorance with the system where we somehow learn - how to set goals but unfortunately, we have no clue about how to set the right goals for life. And in this book, we are going to talk about how to set the right kind of goals.

I am sure by now you must be wondering – what do I mean by setting the right kind of goals? Well, when you learn to set the right kind of goals and work on them in the long run then they set you free from many life's trouble. Let's understand this point with the help of one suitable example. In the year 2007, two young fellows named Mr. Binny Bansal and Mr. Sachin Bansal started an unknown eCommerce company called Flipkart. Yes, I know if you are from India, you know today Flipkart is the same as what Amazon stands for in the USA. They started with zero customers and zero revenue but over the years as per industry estimation now they serve over 12 million active customers each month. They were active members of the company till 2018 when American retail giant Walmart bought it over by purchasing the majority stakes (77%) for a record-breaking by paying $16 billion. Today, both the co-founders are billionaires and living their life as per their choice and interest. They are free to do whatever they wanted to and this is because they **decided to set and work on the right set of goals.** And by the way, both are below 40 years of age at the time of writing and publishing this book.

I hope this incredible Indian story of an eCommerce giant will inspire you to think that yes, there is a huge opportunity to grow in life, and only if we can know how to set right kinds of goals. Let's understand why setting the right kind of goals is important.

Goals Give You Focus In Life

Well, I know this topic is easy to understand. So, we will try to understand this differently. All the great sages, philosophers, and successful people believe that success in life is the direct result of your focus on your goals. The better you can focus and concentrate on your goals better your chances of being successful. Although in the modern world of digitalization, anyone can access any kind of information on the internet. But despite that millions and billions are suffering and spending their time and money without achieving any significant goals. When you lose focus in life you stop growing and reaching your goals and that's the biggest obstacle in people's life. In today's time information is easily available but then people are suffering from information overload.

Today, if I will ask you to search on any topic of your choice on Google, chances are you might see at least thousands of results related to your search. Pieces of information are available in the form of blogs, forums, videos, and audios, etc. Fifteen years ago, we had only three main sources of information – television, radio, and newspaper. Now, we have several other options like – Google, television, radio, WhatsApp, social media sites, podcasts, youtube channels, newspapers, magazines, ebooks, online courses, and many more. Nowadays, you can search for almost anything by using your mobile. That's why despite available information with us we still haven't learned how to reach goals.

When we talk about focus and goals then can we learn to develop a focus in life? Well, the answer is yes and no. To understand this you have to know the difference between interested and committed. If you are really interested to reach your goals then you may learn it. But if you are really committed then definitely you will learn and do it better than any other interested person.

Earlier I had some interest in writing content but nowadays I am more than two hundred percent committed to building my online business by using the content writing formula. For this purpose, I have already decided to write at least five to six books in 2021. And by the grace of God, I will complete writing and publishing my four books by 20th March 2021 on different topics. Remember, when you are focused then you become a powerful weapon like a laser-targeted missile. This is how goals help us to gain focus in life but only when we are fully committed to our goals.

Goals Help You Measure Progress In Life

In the previous topic, we read and understood how do goals help us to stay focused on life. Another amazing thing about the goal is they also help us to measure progress in life. Parag, my very good friend from Rajkot, Gujarat (India) was a young and bright boy in school and he always dreamt of becoming a chartered accountant (CA). To achieve his long-term target he studied hard both in school (Saint Mary, Rajkot) and college. After completing his basic education he studied Bachelor of Commerce (BCOM) from Christ College, Rajkot. Well, now his story gets even more exciting and inspiring. While, most of his friends use to attend college daily, whereas to achieve his dream he did something unusual and I clearly remember it. One day, he wrote a letter to the father (principal) of our college, where he requested him to give a permanent leave as he is interested in appearing in the CA examination. He also clearly mentioned that he will always attend any examination conducted by the college authority and will be a part of this institute only. Although as per the guidelines and rules of university seventy percent attendance is compulsory to be allowed to sit in the examination.

But somehow Parag due to his good character and after a long discussion managed to convince father (principal) that he will take care of his college studies by himself. Later we saw Parag a few times in the college. He used to come but most of the time he used to do self-study and go for CA coaching. If there are around one thousand days in three years of his college life then I think we saw Parag only for a hundred days. Later after many years through another good friend Yashwant Wala we came to know that Parag followed some strict regime for his studies. In the morning after having breakfast he used to enter his study room and close the door. Later he would come out only to take the lunch and then again he would enter the room and study till he will be called for dinner. There was no entertainment and time for him to even play cricket like any other college-going friends. He would spend his entire day and night to complete his rigorous studies. It took him straight four years of hard work, patience, and dedication to achieve his goal and today he is one of the most successful CA among our college batch mates. He was so dedicated in his studies that he learned one of the toughest examinations of India in one go even before he completed his articleship. Those who are familiar with articleship will understand what this means.

Well, if you are thinking is this a real story then yes this is a real story and Parag is my very good friend. He is an ideal hard working person for me who can easily inspire anyone from his life's success story. All these years he kept his eyes only on his goal. And each and every step he took in this journey helped him to measure success and progress in life. When he took commerce in the eleventh standard or when he decided to do BCOM he knew he was going in the right direction. He knew how to measure his progress when he enrolled for the intermediate level CA course and when he did articleship. All these years because he fixed his goals it helped him to measure all his progress in life. Today, I am happy to inform you that he has over fifteen years of experience as a CA and he is currently working with ICICI bank in Ahmedabad (Gujarat), India. If anyone can learn like him to identify his/her goal in the early stages of his school days then he/she can literally achieve their goals. That's how goals help us to measure progress in our life. And nowadays when we talk over the phone then I proudly say to him what he has done and achieved in his career as a CA, and I wanted to achieve something similar to that as an author and digitalpreneur.

Goals Help You to Stay Motivated In Life

By the time when I understood how right goals are important for life, it was already too late, at least as per my age and experience. After I left my highly lucrative job in the year 2012, I suffered tremendously in terms of money, work, emotion, and health. Although I was earning that was nothing in comparison to the salary I was getting paid as a Supervisor in the advertising agency. But

I was determined to leave the corporate rat race behind. I gained such knowledge by reading more number of books. They motivated me to do something different. I was sure that I will not work for someone else for my whole life. I wanted to taste and become a successful entrepreneur.

In the initial stages, I suffered tremendously. I even suffered from brain disease for almost three years, which almost broke my entire condition and dreams. Although I was lucky enough to get married by the age of twenty-eight later even my wife lost all hope and gave me a divorce due to my deteriorating health condition and other family problems. And I don't blame her even one percent for such an outcome. After all, she is working in the Govt. bank and wanted to achieve many dreams. I know I have failed her as a husband. Although I was jobless and suffering from brain disease still, I managed to inform her that she should give me some more time to get well and after that, I will work hard and create some great magic in my life by the use of digital marketing. I learned about the fundamentals of digital marketing in the year 2016 in Hyderabad (India). But I continuously suffered from brain disease from late 2015, 2016, 2017. Only in 2018, I was able to gain my confidence back. I again spent almost the whole of 2018 working as an IT and Soft Skills teacher and I spent the entire 2019 learning different aspects of digital marketing by purchasing many online courses. Since I was already a divorcee by then I decided to try one more time after continuously failing four times as an entrepreneur. But this time I choose digital platforms to launch my business and I opted to become a digital entrepreneur. Now I can do anything for my business by sitting in the comfort of my laptop. I even have a dedicated office to do all my work. I started this journey as a digital entrepreneur in November 2019. And I selected content writing as my powerful weapon to launch my career in this field.

Below are the lists of some of my achievements in 2020 alone:

a) Learned how to design a blog
b) Started a blog related to North East India
c) Wrote at least twenty articles for the blog (yes, I know it is less)
d) Joined Micro Video Mastery group and made 21 videos in straight 21 days
e) Joined online Writopreneurs group
f) Managed to win an article writing contest four times in a row (out of over 500+ members).
g) Managed to write over 1 lakh and 20 thousand (120 thousand) words in a single year
h) Started a YouTube channel with my friend

i) Started writing for the Hubpages forum and wrote 144 articles in eight months

j) Started my freelancing agency and provide services related to content writing, website designing and cover designing, editing, and formatting

k) Able to teach someone online

l) Joined online Authorpreneurs group

m) Managed to write books and

Of course, started making money online. Besides these, I have joined many other groups but not so active in those groups.

Now, I live every day to achieve my goals. All these and more I could achieve because I kept my goals in front of my eyes all this time. Goals helped me to stay motivated and now I have understood how to use content writing to create my own online business even by sitting at home. To reach this goal, I have decided to write, and publish at least five to six books each year till 2023. And then I will teach and offer my system, method, and tools to anyone in my small town. I want to see more writers and authors publishing their books and making money online.

Goals Help You Determine What You Want In Life

There is something amazing energy in your goals if you can feel it. It has been believed that people choose their goals but in reality, dreams and goals choose people as per their desire and as per the energy they vibrate. So, before you make any goals ask whether you have a real strong desire and purpose for that. And when you make goals do you feel the energy and power from inside which can ultimately help you to reach your goals. There is a direct relationship between your goals and wants in life. If you want to purchase a BMW super luxury car then you need to make bigger and better goals in life. You need to expand your visions and possibilities to make more money. If you will not believe and work towards your goals then you cannot able to get what you want in your life. Your goals will decide your directions and actions in your life. Your actions should align with your ultimate goals and then only you can fulfill your dreams, wants, and desires.

So, what do you want from life? Do you want to achieve great success in life? Do you dream of having financial freedom? Do you want to build multiple sources of income? Do you want to be in a great relationship? Do you want a bigger home, a better job, and time to travel the world? Well, first you have to decide what you want from life. Without this, you cannot make great goals. This is the first important step to achieve any goals in life.

Whatever questions I have asked my answer is yes for them. And like any other individual, I am going to work hard day and night and will achieve my set goals one by one. I have seen and visualized success inside my mind thousands of times and now I am going to manifest them. Of course, it may take some time but I am not worried about that. I am going to take massive actions with lots of enthusiasm and will focus all my energy to achieve my set goals.

Now before we move ahead let's understand the three main parts of any goals. These are:
 a) Goals should be specific and time-bound
 b) Aggressive yet realistic &
 c) It should be measurable

Mr. Ravi is interested in writing different books. Let's understand this from an author's point of view. Suppose, he is making a goal to achieve great success by writing books then how is he going to do that? What things he has to take care of and how he is going to measure his success? Keeping the above points in mind, we are going to learn this process step by step. First of all, Ravi realized he is good at writing content and decided to write at least six non-fiction books related to self-development and growth for the coming four years. He also decided to use self-publishing platforms like Amazon Kindle, iBook, Google Play, and Kobo to achieve this target. He decided to use the below-mentioned plan to achieve his set goals.

Step 1 – He decided to join one online course and community of authors
Step 2 – He will learn the entire system and process of writing, publishing
and promoting his books online
Step 3 – He decided to write aggressively one book every two months

Let's assume he can write six books by the end of the year. So, while reviewing his progress at the end of the year he is happy and content with the way he achieved his goals. Now, if you will study this case closely, you will notice that his goals of writing six books was too specific and time-bound i.e six books in 12 months. Not only that he worked aggressively and it was a realistic goal. And since every two months, he was continuously writing, publishing, and promoting his books, he also made over $20,000/- in a year. In this way, he could measure his success and goals both physically and in even monetary terms.

I hope this chapter alone gave you some more insights related to the world of making goals and achieving them. There is a common belief that systems always work and deliver but people fail. But it is also true that only people make systems and use them. So, if you want to become successful in your life and career then learn different systems excessively and use them as much as you can.

Goals Help You To Build Blue Print For Success

Harry wants to earn $20,000 in one year and he decided to use online marketing to reach this target. He is good at copywriting hence, he decided to use content writing and make videos for his YouTube channel. Since Harry is from an advertising background so he decided to use his industry reference to get clients. And as he has also started as a freelancer, he decided to charge $20 for 1500 words articles. His past goodwill worked in his favor and he managed to get work from 10 clients. After some initial projects 5 clients move ahead and hired him on a monthly retainership basis. Now, he is charging $200 per client per month and in this way, he managed to make $12000 in one year from his content writing assignments. Apart from that, he decided to share his knowledge for free by making videos on YouTube. As he shared many good tips, tricks, and honest methods to write content he received a great response from his YouTube community. Slowly and steadily he started making money from his YouTube channel. And before the year ends he managed to make up to $7000. In this way, he managed to make over $19000 in a year which is a little below his target. But a good year for Harry.

Now, if we analyze his success story then we can see some important patterns. First of all, he was too clear about his goal and mission. He knew exactly what he has to do to reach his goal. He decided what tools and techniques he can use. He knew how to market his service and whom to contact. In a nutshell, he prepared his blueprint well in advance. This story also convinces us that planning plays an important role in achieving goals. Many successful people believe that if we can plan well in advance then we can take advantage as we process. Without the right planning and road map, it will be very difficult to decide the next course of action. Once every milestone is fixed then we can easily measure our progress and that's why we need to have fixed goals for life and career.

I hope you have learned something valuable from this lesson alone. I have shared some stories especially of my friend, Parag because whenever I think of achieving goals then somehow I remember his incredible journey. I am always eager to learn his success methods. And during our conversations, I realized his success was the combination of goal setting, focus, and tremendous hard work and never give up attitude in life. As a CA, he is thriving in his career for the last fifteen years and I think there is still fire in his belly.

Chapter 2

Why Do People Fail Despite Goal Setting?

"If you're bored with life – you don't get up every morning with a burning desire to do things – you don't have enough goals"
By Lou Holtz, American Football Player

....

The best part about individual goal setting is you can set standards, time, and pace. If you want to grow fast then increase the amount of hard work and duration of work. An average employee works almost 9 x 6 = 54 to 60 hours in a week. Whereas an average entrepreneur works for almost 12 x 7 = 84 to 90 hours in a week. Yes, some people love to work even on holidays. We all love to set goals and want to achieve them in life. Nobody wants to fail and be known as a failure. Despite this worldwide as per studies, it has been found that the majority of people fail to achieve any significant goals in life. In one study conducted by Scranton University, it has been found out that 92% of people who set any kind of New Year's resolutions fail to achieve any of them. Only 8% of people can achieve their goals. Yes, I know it sounds a little crazy, but when I came to know about this I too couldn't able to believe it initially.

I am writing this book primarily to teach people how to set goals and despite that I also want people to know why do they fail despite setting goals. So many people set amazing goals in life but they fail to achieve them. There must be some reasons and as an author, it is my responsibility to share those facts which can help my readers. In this way, you can learn to avoid them and correct them if you are dealing with them. So, are you someone who set goals but fail to achieve them? First of all, learn to accept this as a fact. Millions and billions of people set goals but fail. It is a normal thing to happen in life. But we need to learn from those mistakes and take appropriate steps. If you are like the majority of people who love to set goals but you fail to reach them despite all efforts then you need to find out the reasons and then learn to take better actions.

There was a time when I used to make big goals and then I will work for some time and then I will fail to achieve them. So, yes, sometimes we do fail to achieve our targets. But from 2019 onwards I changed myself completely and now I am a different kind of person. Since I work online, I make individual goals and I achieve all targets. Now, I can say I am luckier in achieving my goals and targets. But more than luck I would say it is because of hard work and passion. I simply work when others sleep at night. I work when others believe in relaxing and I work when others go out for a party or picnic. I follow my ideal Elon Musk. Well, I work hard with lots of passion and dedication because I have decided to change my life completely by march 2023. Yes, I have given a timeline to myself to achieve my overall goals of life and this book is a small part of that. I hope I have motivated you to achieve your goals. Ok, now let's try to understand why do people fail despite their goals settings, and targets.

People Are Not Serious About Their Life And Goals

James is a young and easy-going student and he believes it is easy to achieve goals in life. His parents want him to study hard, get good marks and get a job in the banking sector. Since James is from a small town, he has no idea about living in the big city but he wanted to go either to Delhi or Bangalore and study in some big college. He is an average student and somehow he managed to pass graduation. So, he decided to go out to Delhi and fill forms for admission to various colleges for his higher studies. He met someone from his state and they started living together as roommates. But unfortunately, since he got less percentage his applications were rejected. So, he decided to study at a private institute. Since it is relatively easy to join a private college, he managed to get admission. But his parents have to pay around Rs. 7,00,00 ($9589) for his two years of study.

Since students don't have the proper industrial exposure before the time of interview many HR experts believe students are not well qualified or trained enough to deserve a higher salary. It is a fact in India as many students end up getting less salary in comparison to what they have spent studying in such colleges. And we are made to believe that in the beginning, it is absolutely alright to get a low salary. Since he is from a small town he had a problem in speaking and writing good English. He faced difficulties related to traveling and often used to reach his office late. And his life's struggles continue for a long. Well, now if we introspect James's life we will notice some common mistakes which many youngsters do.

a) He is not active and serious about his life and career

b) He never made any major goals in his life

Youngsters usually make some random goals in life and they have an attitude that we will see it later when the time will come. And this is the biggest mistake we as a human do. We are fool enough to believe we have ample time with us. If we will not learn to do the right thing at the right time then we will have to face difficulties in the later stages of our life. And I am writing this book when our world is facing a tough situation due to coronavirus and lockdown. Millions and millions of people lost their jobs. Despite that, if we will not learn to become serious about working on the right goals then as an individual we are going to face the disaster. If you have a friend like Parag who says I am going to become CA and works day and night to achieve his goal then you can say he is serious about his life and goal. If you want to be serious about life then learn to work on your individual goals apart from a corporate job. It takes some amount of experience and failure to know more about life. Yes, later we are going to learn about this in more detail.

People Don't Want To Spend Time Working On Goals

The majority of people love to make goals. But then something happens with all of us. One of the biggest excuses I hear from others when they say they are too busy in their job and cannot work on their life's goals. You see we are going to spend the next thirty years of our life working for someone else. But if by chance something will happen to us then the company will not think about us even for ten minutes and we will be replaced by someone else in less than seven days. If you decided to do something about your life then go ahead and do it. Never think it is not possible. I am not asking you to leave your current job. But see this is the biggest truth about any job or career. If you are working for some company remember you can be replaced by anyone else. The only way to save yourself after such a situation is by working and building your own business and in today's time learn to build an online business.

We don't know when and how another pandemic will happen. Are you prepared for such a terrible situation? Have you thought about what are you going to do during those crucial times? I want to tell you seriously during the lockdown in 2020 if you haven't started your online business or learned new skills then you never lacked time but you lacked skills related to planning, dedication, and motivation. I have seen people coming stronger due to lockdown. I have seen online coaches who could sell their online courses to 4000 people in India and able to make over 10 million. I know someone who wrote books and able to become Amazon best-selling author. I know someone who started a YouTube channel and able to start making money within eight months. I know the story of laborers from Majuli, Assam (India), who were able to start mustard cultivation in 100 acres of land. So, what is stopping you to work on your goals? Remember nobody can predict the future but we can continuously work on our dreams and make them big in life.

We Are More Concerned With Other's Opinion

Rohan always wanted to start an eCommerce business and for this purpose, he has taken an online course. He is even sharing his ideas and thoughts related to his project with his close friend, James. Although James is his close friend yet he doesn't endorse his idea since they are yet to graduate. James believes that they should study hard, get good marks and apply for Govt. jobs or in the banking sector as they are more secure in nature. Even Rohan's parents are against his eCommerce startup idea. Since James is Rohan's best friend he decided to trust him more than his ideas, belief, or mentors.

In life, we will always meet people who will tell us that our goals and ideas are impossible to achieve. They are not practical in life and we will be wasting our time, money, and energy. They will say no one in our society has done something like this therefore, we shouldn't try to do it. Unfortunately, Rohan decided to listen to his parents and James. Somehow he lost interest in his ideas and goals. Finally, he decided to study well and get good marks and apply for various Govt. jobs like any other friends of his age group.

Now, before we go ahead and learn something new tell me what should you have done if you were in Rohan's place? If you study Rohan's case closely you will find he had almost everything in place i.e idea, some desire, course, mentor, and financial back from parents. But he lacked in one major area and he used to listen and trust others' opinions and lacked self-believe. For such people, my only advice is don't listen to others. When you have some dreams and goals then you must work on them. Remember, it has been said that people don't choose dreams but dreams choose people as per their abilities. Therefore, during such times it is important to choose to believe in yourself and you need to follow your heart. If Rohan would have tried there could be two outcomes either he would have failed or he would have build a successful business. But even if Rohan would have failed the idea and experience he would have gained will help him to relaunch his business one more time. Don't live your life as per other's expectations. Work for your dreams and one day you will become more successful than other's opinion.

We Try To Accomplish Many Goals At Once

Another biggest mistakes people do related to their goal setting is they try to accomplish too many goals at once. If you try to catch two rabbits at the same time then you will catch neither of them. This is an extremely simple but valuable lesson for life. In life, if you want to accomplish any major goal then you need to have focus and dedication towards that goal. If you desire to become an author then you need to concentrate and devote more time, energy, and money to learn the skills required to become an author. Don't become a jack of all trades and master of none. When I started my digital marketing journey in 2019 I did this mistake, I tried to do too many things. But sooner I realized that I need to focus on one topic. Then I diverted my entire attention to learning more about content writing and how to build a business by using the power of content writing. In 2020, I put my effort into writing articles and by hard work, I managed to write more than 160+ articles. For 2021 and beyond I have decided to write multiple books and I am going to use forums like Medium and Hubpages to expand my content writing business.

Now if you are thinking what is the best way to achieve multiple goals then you need to do something like this. According to me, you should concentrate your entire energy to achieve a single goal until it starts giving good returns in terms of value and money. Once that is set then you can start working on other important goals. First, identify and start to focus all your energy on one goal. It is quite common that people can have multiple goals but you need to start with one goal. Learn to identify what is the most urgent goal from what is less important. Hence, before you start any project or work learn to ask yourself – is this work will help me to reach my big goal and target? If the answer is yes then go ahead and work hard as much as possible. Focus and work on the right goal now.

So, how committed are you to achieving your goals? Are you willing to do and learn everything related to your task? Or you have decided to do what is easy and convenient for you. It has been said if you try to remain normal you will get normal results in life. But if you want powerful and amazing results in life then you need to take powerful actions for that. When it comes to goal achievement, we need to be in control and we need to put in 100% effort. If you will not be serious about life and your goals then you shouldn't dream of achieving them. I know many people who wanted to build an online career and I give them my honest opinion and ideas but then when they reach back home from work, they either spend their time watching Netflix or play video games and after a few months later they will ask the same question to me. When you will become committed towards your set goals then you will wake up by 6 am and ready to push and work till 1 am. Selecting goals and achieving them depends upon your burning desire and commitment towards your life and goals. Remember that you are what you do and not what you say you will do. People believe more in those who take action.

We Get Distracted Easily

Nowadays we can gather information and knowledge from various sources like blogs, podcasts, books, online courses, youtube channels, etc. There is no better time in history to learn new things simply by sitting at home. Online and internet have opened many opportunities for everyone. Both knowledge and entertainment are available at our fingertips. We have learned to do business simply by using mobile and laptop. But along with this human attention span has reduced over time. According to a study conducted by Microsoft, it has been observed that the average human attention span has reduced to just eight seconds. And another fact is people are more interested to enjoy life rather than working on their personal goal. It has also been observed that out of every 100 individuals who make any kind of New Year resolutions only 8 people will complete them. So, why do many people face problems related to this issue?

Many individuals around the world want to become slim and fit and want to reduce their weight. This is one of the most common resolutions which people take every New Year. They even take action, learn some physical exercise but slowly within one month they get distracted. They lose focus and within a few days, they forget about their goals. The problem is the majority of people want easy solutions in their life and when they don't get quick results then they lose interest in the process. Never let such things happen in your life if you are serious about your goals. Achieving any major goals and success takes time. In life, there is nothing like a quick and easy solution. For every goal, you have to work hard with dedication. So, what are the right solutions for this? If you are someone like me who likes to enjoy working from home then certainly I can share some of my important tips. I use them on daily basis and I got great results. Some of them are easy tips but it takes a good amount of daily practice.

Tip No. 1 – *Reduce spending time on social media for more than one hour.* I don't believe in using social media for more than 1 hour a day. If you are not using social media to make money then you shouldn't become addicted to these platforms. Remember and learn to use social media in your favor.

Tip No. 2 – *Learn to work in silence.* Whenever I work on any writing assignments I usually work inside my office. I close my doors and just visualize the outcome and start doing my work one by one. Over time this one habit gave me tremendous results.

Tip No. 3 – *Remove all social media and gaming apps from mobile*. This is an extremely important step for your success. From my mobile, I have removed all such apps be it Facebook, Instagram, Twitter, or LinkedIn. I only use a laptop to check and update my information.

Tip No. 4 – *Always give more importance to goals*. The majority of people do things that are easy and convenient to them. If you will not work hard for your goals and dreams then you will never be able to achieve them. Learn to focus on work and things will change automatically.

Tip No. 5 – *Set a particular time to work and enjoy life*. Although I am not against enjoying life my idea related to entertainment is a little bit different. When I work then I get a lot of high. When I achieve some sort of online success that is my ultimate entertainment and source of inspiration.

Tip No. 6 – *Don't surround yourself with mediocre people*. Either you work completely alone or work with a high-performance team. It is believed that you are an average of 5 people you spend the most time with. If you are working alongside a group of successful writers and authors then certainly you will become one of them sooner or later. Remember success leaves clues and you need to become a good observer.

Tip No. 7 – *Stop multi-tasking.* It is very important to understand that focus gives us direction in life. But then we need to focus on one direction and that will be going to make all the difference. Just like you cannot concentrate on two thoughts at the same time, therefore you should stop multi-tasking and focus only on the main goal.

Chapter 3

How To Set Goals, Progress, And Achieve them?

"If you want to be happy, set a goal that commands your thoughts, liberates your energy and inspires your hopes"
By Andrew Carnegie, Scottish-American Industrialist And Philanthropist

....

I remember when I was in school before any major examination our teachers used to give instructions related to some important topics and chapters. We as normal kids used to take proper notes. During subject revisions, I used to go through those chapters and important topics more often. Sometimes, we used to discuss among friends in great details. In this way, we can easily remember and understand the topics. I remember during the examination I used to study for straight 9 hours in a day. During those times I used to forget to take any kind of food and water. Somehow I used to gather stamina and energy to reach that level.

I am sharing those moments in details because this chapter somewhat reminds me of those days. And I feel this is the most important part of this book. If you will read them well and apply them in the real world then there are high chances for you to achieve your dreams and goals in life. Till now we have understood why setting the right goals is important in life and we have also understood why do people fail despite goal setting. Now is the right time to understand how we can set goals, progress, and achieve them.

It has been observed that people become more active in preparing for their New Year goals by December end. But studies say 67% of people quit within few days and another 25% of people follow their New Year resolutions and goals till February end. Only 8% of people go ahead and do everything necessary to achieve their goals and they become successful individuals in life. So, what is the secret behind their success? Well, first of all, congratulations, actually there is no secret at all, and it is all about proper planning, effective goal setting, dedication, some mentorship, and a lot of hard work. In this chapter, we are going to study 5 methods of goal setting. They are easy to understand and apply. Once you set goals in life that you wanted to achieve then you will love to learn and do everything possible to reach your set destination.

Be Very Specific With Your Goals

Ruby was a young girl with a dream of achieving great success in life. She always wanted to become a doctor. Her parents were ready to help her completely so she can fulfill her dreams. She was a good student and usually used to top in her class. She took science and passed basic education with flying colors. She appeared for medical examination, secured top rank, and got easy admission in one of the most prestigious medical institutes of India. Then she dedicated over five years and earned her medical degree. This is a simple story of many hard-working medical students. In my own family, I have at least six cousins and many relatives who are either engineers and doctors and from their childhood, they are always clear about their career.

While deciding on any kind of goals you have to be very specific with them. Don't make random goals and think of achieving them. For example, if in New Year you have a goal of purchasing a new car then you have to decide everything related to that. You just cannot wish and say I want to purchase a car. But decide exactly which brand, which model, which color, at what price, which showroom, which day you wanted to purchase that car, and how you are going to manage your finance. And if you have decided to take some loan then decide from which bank and what kind of loan you will take i.e personal or car loan etc. The more specific you will become the more clarity you will have in life.

As a writer and an author, this year my goal is to write at least seventy articles for Hubpages forum and six books. To start and complete my journey I have already decided on my author niche, topics of all six books, and I have even decided on topics for the next thirty articles. I have already done basic online research and read about them in my previous year. I have already decided how I will do online marketing and promotion. I know at what price I will launch my book and how to move forward. I know what tools to be used for keyword selection etc. I have decided on when I have to write and complete each book. Mentally, I have already reached my targets now I have to simply move my body and take massive actions. When you decide about your goals make sure you want and love to achieve them. When you do something which you love then it becomes relatively easy for you to push yourself and sacrifice other things in life. If you are an entrepreneur like me and have a burning desire to achieve set goals then you will love to work day and night without ever getting tired.

Set Exciting And Challenging But Achievable Goals

I hope you have understood the previous topic clearly because that is the foundation of any goal setting. If you are not clear about your goals then there will be no focus in life. And without any focus and dedication, you cannot achieve any specific goals. Let's move to the second important aspect of goal setting. But before we move ahead, pause for some time and decide your goal which you wanted to achieve immediately. It can be any goal as per your requirement. You are the master of your life and you have to decide. Now you may be wondering why I asked you to do this exercise? Well, read further and try to answer the below mention questions:

a) Do you get excited after thinking about your goals?
b) Is your goal challenging in nature?
c) Are you ready to invest time, effort, and money?
d) Do you want and love your goals?

If your answer is a big "yes" for all the above questions then I believe you are ready and will do everything to achieve your goals. But if your answer is "big no" then I think you haven't set the right kind of goal. And in this book, we have already discussed this topic (right goals) in detail in the first chapter itself. You shouldn't set that kind of goals that are small and easy to achieve because such goals will not motivate you in the real sense. If you are not ready to leave your comfort zone then don't think of making goals. And in the same way, you shouldn't opt for such big goals about which you already knew are more of fiction than real goals. But there should be a balance, and goals should be big but real and practical.

Let your goals and dreams excite you. Let them make you jump out of bed every day. Set some challenging goals but also make sure they are practical and achievable. We shouldn't decide to achieve those goals about which we already know that it will be not possible anyhow. For example, as an author I cannot make some unrealistic goal i.e. I will write twenty books in a year. Of course, this is a challenging task but definitely, such kind of goals doesn't excite me because I know this is an unrealistic and unpractical goal to achieve. So, I decided to write up to six books this year which I think is exciting and challenging but also practical.

Break Down Your Goals

When I was in college or working in the corporate sector for eight years I had no idea about the concept called multiple sources of income. I was surprised that even my parents haven't heard about these terms. Nowadays there are many youngsters who are aware of this concept called multiple income streams. And the best part is they are hungry and doing everything possible to make this a reality. Since they have learned about this concept they have also learned that although they have multiple goals they are focusing on only one goal in the beginning.

Now let's go deeper and jump into more practical ways to achieve our goals. There are many methods to break down goals but I am going to share a simple and effective method that I apply to achieve my goals. There is an interesting phrase that says – *"how do you gonna eat an elephant?"* and the answer is – one bite at a time. In the same way, the goal which looks gigantic and big like a dinosaur we need to break down our goals into smaller goals. For example, if you are a writer and author and if you have decided to write at least six books this year then you should write one book each every two months. And by using today's technology it is possible to write, publish and promote books by becoming a self-publishing author. So, an author can use the technique mentioned below:

Jan-Feb	Mar-Apr	May-June	July-Aug	Sept-Oct	Nov-Dec
1st Book	2nd Book	3rd Book	4th Book	5th Book	6th Book

Now, if you wanted to know is it possible to write a book in two months? Well, in my own experience I would say yes it is possible to write a non-fiction book within 30 days or less. This step also fulfills our second step i.e exciting, challenging and practical goal. Deciding on goals and achieving them is a long process. It takes time, effort, money, and full dedication.

Design A Step By Step Action Plan

Before we develop a step by step action plan we have to see what all changes we have to bring in our life to achieve our goals. We cannot achieve targets simply by planning if we are not ready to make changes in the way we work and think. Sometimes in life and career, new goals mean we need to do something new. Before we decide on an action plan we need to see what habits we need to build. What kind of discipline do we need to have? Are you ready to do the hard work? Are you willing to work till late at night and ready to get up as soon as possible? Are you ready to push yourself every day? What daily routines will you follow? Life is unpredictable and complicated, so are you ready for that? We need to see many things before we make a detailed action plan.

We need to break down our goals and go much deeper step by step as mentioned in the diagram below. For this purpose, we are taking the example of writing six books in a year. You can call this part preparing your step-by-step baby steps.

How To Create A Step By Step Weekly And Daily Action Plans?			
Yearly Goals	**Monthly Goals**	**Weekly Goals**	**Daily Goals**
To write six books in a year	Write one book each every two months	Write one chapter each week	Write at least 500 to 1000 words each day
Note: if you will follow these steps one by one then it will be easy for you to reach your milestones. I am also sure that anyone can reach their goals before expected timeline.			

In this method, we have learned how to go much deeper and how to plan weekly and daily routines. If you ask me regarding goals, I would say I don't believe in yearly goals or resolutions. I only believe in weekly and daily goals. And based on this, I make my yearly goals. Let's understand the reasons why having step-by-step weekly or daily action plans are more important to achieve goals.

a) It will be easy for you to monitor the process and progress

b) You can focus on the most important task

c) You can spend more time with better dedication

d) When you plan better and in detail, you can decide faster and better

e) It will be easy for you to evaluate the day and week

f) It will help you to reach your monthly and yearly target more easily

There are many techniques which many productive people like Bill Gates and Elon Musk use. Time blocking is one such technique. It is very easy to use and we have used this technique for many years during our school and college days. I hope you remember something called a time-table, through which we know exactly at what time which subject we have to attend and study.

Example Of Time Blocking = Time Table						
Time	Mon	Tue	Wed	Thur	Fri	Sat
8 to 12 am	RE and WR	RES	RE and WR	RE and WR	Visit Bank	RE and WR
1 to 2 pm	Lunch	Lunch	Lunch	Lunch	Lunch	Lunch
3 to 4 pm	ME and Email	ME and Email	Idea Generatio n	ME and Email	RES	Editing & Design
4 to 5 pm	Tea Break	Tea Break	Tea Break	Tea Break	Tea Break	Tea Break
5 to 8 pm	Work	Work	Work	Work	Work	Work

8 to 9 pm	Dinner	Dinner	Dinner	Dinner	Dinner	Dinner
9 to 11 pm	Work	Work	Work	Work	Work	Work

RE = Reading, WR = Writing, RES = Research, ME = Meeting

If you are thinking does anyone work between 9 to 11 pm. Well, the answer is yes, many online entrepreneurs do work online even after taking dinner. And this is another reason why do people become successful online. By the way, if you are thinking about why Sunday is missing from the time-table then we will keep that day for taking some rest and recharge our batteries. You can design your time-table (time blocking) as per your requirement.

Evaluate And Make Adjustments In Your Goals

One very important aspect of goal setting is you have to understand the difference between a success list and just a to-do list. If you notice the previous diagram under time blocking some points fall under - to-do list like dinner, lunch, and tea break. Whereas work, reading, meeting, idea generation, and editing, designing are our success list. We need to concentrate and focus more on our success list on daily basis. These are related to goals and targets. As we start working on our day-to-day plans many times it may happen that things may not work out as per our plan. During such time we need to evaluate and adjust according to our goals. Remember to change the strategy but don't change your goal. When we travel and face some difficulty during our journey we don't return to our home. We just evaluate and try to adjust as per the situation. Therefore, we can apply the same principles for our life and career goals.

Another example - if you are in the manufacturing industry and are not getting proper raw material from the current supplier then you don't close your factory. You go out and look for some other supplier. If you need money for your business, you will apply for a loan. And if one bank will reject your application then you will visit another bank or look out for investors who can finance your project. So, every time you face a problem, setback and some difficulties study the situation and change some game plan and strategies but never change your goals and targets. I had a goal and big dream that one day I will become a successful entrepreneur but I faced a lot of difficulties in my previous offline businesses. So, this time when I again started my journey as an entrepreneur I choose to become a digital entrepreneur. My goal was, is, and will always remain the same that I wanted to become an entrepreneur but I changed my strategy from offline to online.

Chapter 4

Successful Habits To Achieve Any Goals

*"Obstacles are those frightful things you see
when you take your eyes off your goals"*
By Henry Ford, American Industrialist

....

What would you do if your LED bulb in your house become dysfunctional? Well, most of us would throw it out and purchase the new one, right? But not the Rohit Bhattacharjee, a small-town guy from Algapur, Tripura (India). He is a student of English honors and has set up RB illuminations company just before coronavirus lockdown. He was so determined to get his success that he sold his bike to raise funds for his venture. Today, he has employed seven people and sells around 500 units of LED bulbs a day, and he is earning 2.5 lakh (over $3400) a month.

In his own words - *there weren't too many components, and understanding their role in illuminating the bulb was the only challenge. "The drivers, cap, chip, and body were its main elements, and their capacities differed. None of the components needed any processing, but they did demand careful assembling.*

I thought that instead of buying a new one, why not set up a unit to manufacture LED bulbs altogether".

In the initial stage, Rohit faced difficulty regarding raising funds for his venture as both of his parents were retired government teachers. So, he sold off his bike at Rs. 65000($890) and his parents managed to give him Rs. 3.5 lakh ($4794) from their savings. He used to watch many videos on YouTube and later he managed to source components and types of equipment from vendors in Delhi (India). After a few attempts, he managed to assemble an LED bulb on his own and made the first 50 all by himself. Today, his efforts are being appreciated by the government at the ministry level.

As human beings, we all desire to achieve some major goals and dreams in life. Planning is just one part of goal setting. Once the initial planning is done then we need to build a strong base based on powerful habits. Without strong habits as the foundation we cannot crush our goals and set the high standard. In this chapter, I am going to bust some myths related to how to achieve bigger and more ambitious goals of life.

We all believe and we have been taught that to achieve important goals of life we need to build powerful habits and skills. We need to take some massive action. Need to learn many skills fast. Right?

Well, the truth is to achieve any significant goal in life you don't need much skill. Skills are by-products of your habits. The only things which you need are –

a) How do you approach the problem?
b) What process and habits you build over time?
c) What tools do you use to reach your goals? And most important...
d) What decisions do you take to reach your goals?

In real life, **tiny results** are more important to achieve bigger goals. What kind of **marginal improvement and adjustment** you do on a day-to-day basis will reflect in your long term results. Always remember achieving goals are not a one-day affair. You need to improve the way you work continuously. We need to build many good habits. And more than a spectator and thinker you have to continuously work.

Do we need to build some super successful habits to reach our goal? If so, what are those habits and how can we build them over time? Let's see them one by one.

Proper Time Management

If there is one habit that can change your outcome in the short and long run then my first advice will be related to time management. A person might be highly talented but if he is not good with time management then there is no scope for him. What is the use of that talent if he is not able to finish exams on time, cannot reach the office on time, and attend meetings on time.

On the other hand, if an average guy is always consistent and keeps on improving then in the long run he will progress much better in life. Those people who can master the art of time management can learn any skill and devote better time to progress in life. Many people also say there is time for everything but this is also not true. When you see successful people enjoying, dancing, and having a good time then you forget that before that they gave their best in whatever field they are into and they have actually spent sleepless nights and hours working hard.

There are the following benefits of proper time management:

a) You will be more efficient and productive at work
b) It will help you to improve the quality of your life
c) You will overcome procrastination
d) You can easily start and deliver work and projects on time
e) Your reputation will increase at work
f) You will get more time for recreation
g) You can plan your next assignment much better

Now to improve this habit you have to do regular planning and you need to prioritize your work. There is a misconception that if we want to get better and faster results then we need to do multi-tasking. Yes, it is true that to become successful we need to learn and do many things but we need to focus on one particular area. For example, if you are a blogger then you have to select one particular niche and keep on working and sharing content around one particular area. You just cannot say – I am a food blogger, I am a travel blogger, I am a sports blogger and I am a techno blogger. In the same way, stop multi-tasking and focus on key result areas. Just learn to schedule your task and make sure you start and complete your task as per your time table. Track your time as to where and how you spend your entire day and then start adjusting based on your observations.

Take Proper Rest

Proper rest means going to bed on time and wake up on time. Many people believe to become successful we have to work day and night. Although this is true, but wherever you are you will always have 24 hours in a day. How well you use them depends upon you and your planning. If you will work for long hours then you may not be in the position to work properly the next day. Your body and brain need proper rest to recharge them. If you look into the habits of any successful people you will notice most of them wake up early in the morning. They go out and do some exercise or do some physical exercise in the gym.

Unless you have some urgent projects to complete on time it is always advisable to sleep by 11:00 pm. Next day get up as early as 4:30 am or by 5:00 am, plan your whole day, and start working as soon as possible. If you start your work in the morning, you are more likely to progress and complete it on time. As there will be less disturbance, no social media, no kids around, and no phone calls. It is a great achievement that while others are still sleeping you are taking action as a leader. When you will do that on the regular basis you will neither feel tired or fatigue. Let's see what are the benefits of proper rest.

a) It helps you in improving your memory
b) It will reduce your stress including any headache
c) When you take proper rest your mood will improve
d) You can think clearly and can do more task with ease
e) It will help you improve your focus
f) You can easily work a full day and
g) You feel healthy and energetic

From today onwards, make sure you go to bed on time and wake up every day on time. This one habit will give you much better results in life and you will reach your goals one by one.

Work In Silence

Have you ever noticed why so many successful people love peace and tranquility? It has been observed that to do great things in life we need to focus and that focus we can develop only by working in silence. We are bombarded with two kinds of noise on daily basis. One is excessive noise which is unbearable for some people like the noise of the fast-moving train. And on the other hand, we hear noises on an everyday basis like conversations with colleagues, horns and loud music, etc. Both kinds of noise are bad for our health in the long run. Some studies proved that there is a direct link between noise, sleep loss, lack of focus, and depression, etc.

One study was conducted in Munich where they studied children who went to school near the airport before and after the airport was located. During the research, it has been found out that most students attending that school performed worse on the long-term memory and reading comprehension tests when the airport was near their school.

Later when the airport was moved, it was found that students of nearby schools were performing better on long-term memory and reading comprehension.

I have shared one real-life example with you because I wanted to tell you how excessive noise and sound can damage our performance in the long run. To achieve more success we need to build better habits and work in a better environment. Since, I am a digital entrepreneur, writer, and author I love to work in silence. To achieve my goals I have dedicated one particular room and whenever I have to write articles or content for the next book I simply keep mobile in the silent mode and close the window. Then I simply do some research, understand the topic and I just start writing and writing. In this way, I was able to write more than 140+ articles and win writing content four times in a row.

Some major benefits of working in silence:

a) We can think with better clarity
b) We can do more task with ease
c) We can put our best efforts during silence
d) We can design and plan things better
e) We can do more creative work
f) Easy to understand things faster and better

Once you will understand the power of silence you will always desire to have it. Work in silence and let your results make all the noise. Learn anything required to achieve your goals.

Get Some Help

If you want to go quickly, go alone. But if you want to go far, go together. First of all, we have to understand that whatever problems we are facing right now there is a high possibility that someone might have gone through the same issues. In fact, in today's time, it is easy to meet someone over the internet than having a face-to-face conversation. Chances are nowadays you can meet your next coach, mentor, or teacher online. In today's world some people are eager to teach others and ready to share their life's experience. When you are beginning your journey in any field it is always good to take help and guidance from an experienced person. When you will make mistakes they can offer you the right solutions and help. You can easily overcome problems of life if you just follow their instructions.

I decided to start my journey and become a writer and an author because of two main reasons. First, I found my true love in creative writing, and second, I got better guidance from other writers and many author friends. When you become a part of a bigger group where people are like-minded and think and act the same way then you can learn many things quickly by observing others. I started writing more articles by observing others and I am going to write many books because I truly wanted to achieve my dreams.

Before we move ahead we have to understand something very important related to mentorship. Taking online courses and having a mentor is not a guarantee that you will achieve success. Yes, there is no guarantee. Offline mentors or online teachers can only guide you and give you access to their courses. It is you who have to walk the path individually. I know many people who have taken many online courses. But you will be surprised that only 8 to 10% of people start and complete the course and take some major actions. Nowadays you can easily learn anything online by sitting at your home. You might have the exact blueprint with you but if you are not ready to take some actions you will not get the results. Become a part of some meaningful groups, observe them, learn from them, take suggestions from a mentor and start implementing things fast.

Track Your Progress

It may be possible that we have planned our goals exceptionally well. To achieve any significant goals in life we need to plan in detail. We need to have in-depth clarity about our goals. It is common in human nature to have many targets in life. It is also true that many of us are good at planning but weak in execution and taking real-time action. Action will speak louder than words and only those people who can match their action with words and planning will succeed in life. So, are you one of them? And how can you make sure that you are moving in the right direction? For this purpose, we need to understand and learn to observe our progress. As we have already learned about the importance of making daily, weekly and yearly goals. We just need to track our progress by keeping those goals in mind.

Benefits of tracking our progress in life:

a) We can easily identify our problems and issues
b) We can give more focus and attention to important tasks
c) It can help us in breaking bigger goals into smaller steps
d) We can easily manage more task as we can track our day-to-day work
e) We can gain more confidence and bring discipline in our life
f) Help us in prioritizing our daily work

In simple words, tracking our work helps us to stay more focused on what's important for reaching our goal. By minimum observations, we can easily identify our potential obstacles and barriers. Then based on that, we can set realistic goals and stay more positive and focused along the way. Now, let's understand how we can track our progress related to any projects.

1) **Pareto Principle** - We can use the famous technique called Pareto Principle. According to this, we need to prioritize our work. It is believed that 80% of the effect of our work will come from 20% of the work we do. In simple words, there are some major tasks which if we do sincerely we can get 80% of our results. Therefore, we need to prioritize and focus more on such work. We can apply this technique in our day-to-day tasks also.

2) **Make A To-Do List** - Always write your daily goals. Set a particular time to start and finish your work. Highly productive people always make a list known as – to-do list. There is a myth that we need to write everything on that list. But the reality is we need to include only the most important task which will give us 80% of our results.

3) **Accountability Partner** – Whenever you will start working on any assignment or any major project it will be better if you make someone your accountability partner. They can ask questions related to your progress and you have to reply to them with accurate information. I have made my business partner my accountability partner. I also share my goals in social media, so I will be morally responsible to achieve my targets on time.

I hope now you have understood what kinds of solid habits we have to build in order to achieve maximum targets and goals in life. In the beginning, they may look difficult but once you start practicing these every day you will thoroughly enjoy the entire process. In the nutshell,

a) Time Management
b) Take Proper Rest
c) Work In Silence
d) Get Some Help
e) Track Your Progress

Chapter 5

5 Types Of Goals Every Individual Should Set

"You are never too old to set another goal or to dream a new dream"
By C. S. Lewis, British Writer

....

When Delight was young he set goals related to his studies. His parents advised him to study hard, get good marks and sit in as many competitive examinations and secure a job in the government department. He followed their advice and expected society's norm. But instead of getting a government job, he got a job in the corporate sector, thanks to his higher studies and friend's circle. Every day by 6:00 am he would get up, eat breakfast, and rush to reach his office. He spends more than two hours commuting and another nine hours of his life working for the company. He got regular promotions and even got married and have children. After marriage, he decided to purchase a car, home, and many other things. For this purpose, he took huge personal and home loans. Now he has to work even harder to repay that huge loan and even his wife took a part-time job. Sometimes, he will face complicated issues in the office which will bother him for many days and months. Sometimes, there will be unexpected issues in his personal life. In this way, they spend their entire life working for someone else and never got any chance to work upon their personal goals. And even their kids followed a similar path.

This is the actual life's journey which many of us are going through right now. People like us are a part of a system known as the corporate rat race, where we will be working for companies for our whole life. Someone has nicely said - ***your salary is the bribe they give you to forget about your dreams.*** Although this is true I don't fully agree with this statement. My personal view is every individual should start their career by working for someone else for a few years. He should get some real-life corporate experience and side-by-side he should study how he can set himself free from the corporate rat race as soon as possible.

To become free we need to fully understand the types of goals that we need to set. If you will value and identify these five major goals and start working on them as soon as possible then you can be certain to have a great life ahead. I call them five elements of goals and now let's understand them one-by-one.

a) Career And Professional Goals
b) Health and Fitness Goals
c) Personal Growth Goals

d) Financial Goals

e) Spiritual Goals

I am writing this book related to how we can achieve our goals, so, I am going to share my exact list of goals keeping 2021 as the base year. I am writing and publishing this book in January 2021. I hope anyone who will read this book and follow me on social media will know exactly whether I could achieve my goals or not. And I am going to do that because I wanted to prove to people that anyone with the right mindset, planning, dedication, mentorship, and proper time management can do it. As I have already mentioned five types of goals that every individual should set, therefore, I will be sharing different goals keeping these points in mind. If you will work and achieve these goals in life then you will have more name, fame, money, satisfaction, and most important you will get peace of mind. Individually, each goal is interconnected with each other and you have to work upon them. You have to understand the significance of each of them. Allow me to share some details related to my goals keeping five elements of goals in mind.

Career And Professional Goals

By profession, I am an author, full-time writer, and digital entrepreneur. My key strengths are content writing and designing. I entirely work from home and I stay in a small remote town in India. In late 2019, I decided to leave my job permanently as a teacher and I selected to devote my entire time to build my new career in digital marketing and I choose content writing. In 2020 alone, I wrote more than 140+ articles for the Hubpages forum. I am a member of the writers' and authors' community and by writing continuously, I won a writing contest four straight times in a row. During this time I started one youtube channel with my friend and we are making videos and uploading them each month. Apart from these, we also work for our clients. Those were some of my career goals that I was able to achieve last year. Let me share my career and professional goals for 2021 and beyond. There are five major goals that I wanted to achieve by the end of this year.

- ✓ Work with five clients
- ✓ Focus on learning in-depth SEO
- ✓ Write seventy articles in forums like Hubpages, and Medium
- ✓ Write and publish in total six books in different categories

As I have mentioned if you will stay connected with me through social media you can easily find out whether I could achieve them or not. At the end of this book, there are links related to my social media profiles. So, I hope you will love to stay connected with me.

Health And Fitness Goals

As I have already mentioned that each goal is connected. When we talk about health and fitness then we have to remember that unless you stay healthy you cannot achieve your professional goals. Health is wealth and we need to understand the importance of each goal. There is a direct relationship between health and career goals of life. And when we talk about fitness it is not just about physical activity but it is also related to mental state. So many people are physically fit but mentally they are suffering. To become mentally fit we should know how to relax and how to increase the effectiveness of the mind. For this purpose, it is important to use our brain daily. We need to do some creative activities, play sports like chess, and we should read books and write on daily basis. So, below are the list of my health and fitness goals.

- ✓ Walk 8 km daily
- ✓ Skipping for 10 minutes
- ✓ Reduce weight up to 78 kgs
- ✓ Drink more lukewarm water daily
- ✓ Increase intake of fruits and salads on diet
- ✓ Reduce dairy and animal products from food up to 95%

Personal Growth Goals

Now there is a third kind of goal which is known as personal goals. And as the name itself suggests this goal is personal. You wanted to try them because of your curiosity, hobbies, or interest. When you do them they give you more inner satisfaction and happiness. For example, there are the vast majority of people living in the urban jungle and they are fed up with working in the big cities. They want to leave their high-paying jobs and return to their native place. They all are interested in starting their new career in agriculture. Yes, there are many success stories related to personal growth like this. I know someone closely who left his high-paying corporate job and started mushroom cultivation and today they are one of the best mushroom cultivators of India. Now along with their regular mushroom cultivation, they have started an online course based on their experience.

When we talk about personal growth it doesn't mean you have to leave your current job and start your venture. It means you have to do something which gives you inner happiness, and satisfaction, and which can help you to grow better in your life. But if you can start something of your own which later you can convert into full-grown business then nothing will be better than this. But if you are working for some company then learning new skills and habits which can increase your prospects in a career than it is also a part of personal growth. Below is the list related to my personal growth.

- ✓ Start a personal blog
- ✓ Read in total seven books related to self-development
- ✓ Learn how to start gardening in the backyard
- ✓ Create and share more podcast episodes on Social Media i.e Facebook
- ✓ Create more videos for the YouTube channel

Financial Goals

I believe working on financial goals is one of the most important goals we can have. Since we are living in a society that is driven by the economy we need to have sufficient money to live a meaningful life. It is not that money can buy everything but yes money can buy at least 90% of things you want from life. And that is why this is an important aspect of life. I have attended many online webinars of many financial gurus. Most of them said one thing in common – *we all lack money in life, not because of skills or education but because we lack strong financial education.* And it is a horror to know that generation after generation people are suffering because of this reason. When I was in college or working for corporate, nobody told me about the following aspects related to finance.

- Why financial literacy is important?
- How to attain financial freedom by the age of 35 or 40?
- How to create multiple streams of income?
- How to save yourself from inflation?
- How to start a side hustle with minimum investment?
- Power of digital marketing and social media in building your finance
- How to manage your finance like a pro?
- How to invest or start trading in the stock market?

I learned about them too late but now I am fully determined to learn many things in this regard. To reach my destination, I have already selected my guru and will follow his advice for many years. So, to accomplish some of my financial goals I have selected the following goals.

- ✓ Save and invest 30% of my all earnings every two months
- ✓ Learn how to invest in the stock market
- ✓ Read books related to finance and investment
- ✓ Take an online course related to the stock market
- ✓ Create a new account and save another 10% of my income
- ✓ Create at least three streams of income by year-end

Spiritual Goals

Most people think when we talk about spiritual goals they are related to religious goals. Well, there is a big difference between religion and spirituality. Spirituality is related to your relationship between you and your God. You are a spiritual person when you see all living beings as equal and treat them as equal. When you decided to help others without thinking about their caste, religion, race, or country. When a person becomes spiritual he can see divinity in all living things. It is a different feeling altogether. Well, my idea related to spirituality may be different from yours. But I hope you have understood the meaning. Here is the list of my spiritual goals for this year.

- ✓ Donate 5% of my income to - The Earth Saviours Foundation
- ✓ Feed street dogs as much as possible

Final Conclusion

You can do anything if you set goals. You just have to push yourself.

RJ Mitte

First of all, I highly appreciate and congratulate you and I want to thank you from the bottom of my soul for purchasing and reading my book. To be honest it is an honor. It is the duel effort of an author and his lovely readers who make any book meaningful, original, and successful. And I am so blessed to find you as my valuable reader.

You made it till the end. I sincerely hope you are thinking and feeling bolder than your prior self. It is my honest attempt to show the world that it is possible to achieve any meaningful goals if we are strong enough to take action. And I am committed to use this system which I have mentioned in different chapters. If I will not do what I preach and endorse it will have no real meaning.

We started our whole journey by understanding why setting the right goals are important for life then we also learned why do people fail despite goals setting.

Then we moved towards the core of this book and understood everything related to how to set goals and how to achieve them in life. Here we emphasized why there is a need to have clarity about our goals and why we need to break them down step-by-step. I hope after reading this chapter alone you got many insights that can help you to achieve your goals.

I assure you that I have used them personally and I found them very useful in my day-to-day task. Later we learned about the core successful habits of successful achievers and the five most important types of goals that every individual should set.

The objective of this book will not complete if you will not take any further actions. Some of the ideas and concepts shared in this book may look a little difficult but trust me once you will use them then it will slowly become a part of your daily life.

I am a living example of these systems which I have shared in this book. But before you take any step further, I like to confirm that it takes time, effort, and of course some effort to see sustainable results in the long run.

Here, I like to say that you have now equipped yourself with more wisdom needed to improve the quality of your life by achieving your goals. Take suitable decisions and change your life.

Rest believe in your ability to learn new things and most importantly enjoy every moment. I hope you'll use some of the suggestions compiled in this book. I would be very happy to know how these ideas and suggestions have helped you to transform your life in any manner. With you forever in your struggle, growth, and success.

Cheers,

Vikram Brahma
(Author)

May I Ask You For A Big Favor?

At the very outset, I want to give you a big thanks for taking out time to read this book. You could have chosen any other book, but you took mine, and able to read my book and I totally appreciate this.

I hope you got at least a few actionable insights that will have a positive impact on your day to day life. These ideas and systems which I have mentioned in this book are working for many including me. I sincerely hope you will learn more about them and implement them in your life. Can I ask for 30 seconds more of your time?

I'd love it if you could leave a review of the book. Reviews may not matter to big-name authors; but they're a tremendous help for new authors like me, who don't have many followers. They help me to grow my readership by encouraging folks to take a chance on my books. I promise you to bring more such helpful and insightful books in future.

To put it straight, reviews are the lifeblood for any author. It will just take less than a minute of your time, but will tremendously help me to reach out to more people, so please leave your review. Thanks for your love and support of my work. And I'd love to see your review.

About The Author

"If you haven't failed lately, then you're not learning lately, it's time to challenge yourself with bigger goals and ambitions"
By Vikram Brahma, Author, Writer, Blogger, YouTuber

Vikram Brahma was born in Jammu (India), near the famous Raghunath temple dedicated to Lord Ram. During his school and college days, he was an active athlete and won many awards in sports, drawing, debate, and essay writing competition. Due to his positive nature and alertness, he was selected as the next head boy (KV Uppal No. 1, Hyderabad). He did his post-graduation in Advertising and Communication from EMPI, Business School, Delhi.

He is now a full-time writer and digitalpreneur who loves to work from home. He loves to start his work as early as 7:30 am. He started his online career by designing a blog related to North-East India. Later he realized that he has a special gift of writing a lot of content. In 2020 alone, he wrote more than 1 lakh and 20 thousand (120 thousand) words professionally which includes 167 articles, out of which 144 articles belongs to the Hubpages forum. Due to this special talent, he has managed to win an online article writing contest four times in a row. And the best part is he is still hungry to write more.

Apart from being a blogger, he is a full-time writer, content creator, part-time YouTuber, part-time podcaster, stock investor, and now a published author. Currently, he is writing more books for entrepreneurs and student communities on topics related to productivity, self-development, time-management, and growth. Apart from writing serious content, he has a great interest and love in writing books for children category. He has visualized the power of content writing and he believes that by using his high-income skill he can literally build multiple sources of income within two years.

Overall, he has more than a decade of working experience out of which eight years he has spent working in various reputed advertising agencies. He started his career from RK SWAMY/BBDO and worked in various capacities in different agencies like McCann, Multiplier (Mudra), and Dentsu. He even worked as an IT and Soft Skills teacher, where he gave more than 60 motivational lectures. Apart from that he is a biker by heart and loves to observe others and learn from them. He loves to read a lot of things and even has a collection of over a hundred books through which he keeps on learning and getting inspiration.

He believes that online platforms can literally change the way people work, think, read, and learn. There are huge opportunities out there and anyone who can understand the fundamentals of this can grow and earn millions. He hopes sooner or later people will realize its importance in their life.

So, let me know what you think about writing, digital marketing, and its scope? If you want to stay connected with me through social media you can connect with me in the following ways:
Facebook: https://www.facebook.com/vikram.brahma/
Linkedin: https://www.linkedin.com/in/vikram-brahma/
Instagram: https://www.instagram.com/talesofvikram/

Currently, he is living happily with his proud parents in a small town in Assam (India). He is looking forward to writing and publishing more books in the future. And at last, always remember you're awesome.

Copyright@ 2021 By Vikram Brahma

9 798599 918004